# The Ultimate Frittata

# Cookbook

### Creative Frittata Recipes You Should Try Out

## By: Owen Davis

›>><<‹o›>><<‹o›>><<‹o›>><<‹o›>><<‹o›>><<‹

# Copyright Notice!

›>><<‹°›><<‹°›><<‹°›><<‹°›><<‹°›><<‹

# Table of Contents

# Introduction

Not everyone has adequate time to prepare freshly made meals at home. The busy lifestyle has made people rely more on ready-made food in the nearby food outlets instead of preparing the meals at home. Well, this shouldn't be your case because you don't need hours in your kitchen to make scrumptious frittatas. If you have been searching for that one cookbook that will guide you in preparing a wide range of frittatas for different occasions, you have found the right option. With an open stove, an oven, or even an air fryer, you can make the best frittatas ever and share with others with love.

However busy your schedule might be, you will need something to eat at some point. The banana frittata is a perfect recipe you can serve for breakfast and pack some for your workplace. Try our ramen noodle frittata and experience the magic of combining cheese, eggs, and pasta to make a fulfilling meal. You can even enjoy our shrimp or prawn frittata for dinner when you want something super delicious yet easy to make with basic ingredients. Veggies play a key role in our well being. Try the wide range of veggie frittatas and nourish your skin and overall health. Be it mushrooms, spinach, asparagus, artichokes, or broccoli, among many others, you can always transform them into a healthy meal. Don't forget to try the different mini-frittatas, too, for easy portioning and packaging, especially when you want to carry some or store some in the fridge.

Don't just live; instead, embrace a healthy lifestyle with healthy living habits by making freshly made frittatas at home! The main secret is making this cookbook your number-one kitchen companion.

# Frittata Cooking Tips

As you begin the journey of making delightful frittatas, bear the following tips and tricks in mind. They will help you throughout the process, ensuring you get the best frittatas in the end.

**Know the right cheese.**

Depending on the ingredients you are using to make your frittata, selecting the appropriate cheese is a key concern. This will help give your frittata the right texture and finishing.

**Pro tip**: parmesan is best when sprinkled over cooked eggs, while gruyere and cheddar are best for melting down with the eggs through the cooking process. Feta, when blended with Greek, gives frittata a perfect flavor.

**Don't overbake**

Of course, once the frittata is set, it shouldn't take more than 30 minutes in the oven, depending on the quantity. After all, you need soft textures and moist frittata full of flavors and aromas from the seasonings you used.

**Pro tip**: For a perfectly browned top, you can spread some cheese on top during the last minutes of baking. Again, you can choose to broil the frittata for about 4 minutes after settling in the skillet on an open stove.

**Cook the add-ins first.**

If you are using leftovers, then you are good to go. However, when using fresh ingredients, make sure you cook the add-ins first to ease the cooking process.

**Pro tip**: Make sure you cut the add-ins into small pieces for easy blending with other frittata ingredients. Add-ins are ingredients such as mushrooms, broccoli, and tomatoes, among many others.

**Don't be mean with seasoning.**

Of course, you need a tasty and flavorful frittata. Therefore, add appropriate seasoning to the eggs for perfect blending with other ingredients to get that awesome flavor and taste.

**Choose the right pan.**

The material, the shape, and the size of the pan or skillet you are using play a key role in defining the final frittata results. A cast iron skillet, for instance, will give you a traditional touch. Again, when using the cast iron skillet, remove the frittata from over early since the cooking process will continue; a cast iron skillet keeps heat for a while.

**Pro tip**: using a large, non-stick, oven-safe dish will work magic.

# 1. Green Chile Frittata

Filled with cottage cheese, you can enjoy this delicious frittata for breakfast or brunch. Always preheat in a microwave and serve while still warm.

**Serving Size:** 10

**Cooking Time:** 50 Minutes

**Ingredients:**

- 10 beaten eggs
- ½ cup all-purpose flour
- 1 tsp. baking powder
- Salt as desired
- 16 oz. cottage cheese, low-fat
- 1 cup Cheddar cheese, shredded
- 7 oz. green chile peppers, drained & diced
- ¼ cup melted butter

**Instructions:**

Put the oven settings to 400 degrees F, then butter a 9 by 13-inch baking casserole

Combine salt, baking powder, flour, and eggs in a bowl, then stir in melted butter, chile peppers, cheddar cheese, and cottage cheese; add this mixture into the baking casserole.

Bake in the ready oven for 15 minutes, then reduce the settings to 325 degrees F and bake for 40 more minutes.

# 2. Ramen Noodle Frittata

Are you thinking of a perfect lunch idea filled with noodles? Well, make this frittata, and your kids will love every single bite!

**Serving Size:** 4

**Cooking Time:** 15 Minutes

**Ingredients:**

- 6 oz. chicken flavored ramen noodles
- 6 eggs
- 2 tsp. butter
- ½ cup shredded Cheddar cheese

**Instructions:**

Cook the noodles as per the package guidelines, but keep the seasoning pack. Drain the noodles once cooked.

Whisk together the seasoning packs from the noodles, and eggs, then mix with the noodles.

In a pan set on medium heat, melt the butter, then add the spiced noodles to cook on low heat until firm, about 7 minutes.

Flip to cook on the other side for 2 minutes, then serve sprinkled with cheese.

# 3. American Frittata

Easy to prepare, yet a delicious and nutritious frittata for the whole family. You can as well use sausages in this recipe.

**Serving Size:** 8

**Cooking Time:** 15 Minutes

**Ingredients:**

- 4 cubed potatoes, peeled
- ½ sliced onion
- 1 tbsp. vegetable oil
- 8 beaten eggs
- ¾ cup cubed ham
- salt and pepper to taste
- ¾ cup shredded Cheddar cheese

**Instructions:**

Cook your potatoes in boiling water with salt until al dente, for 5 minutes, then drain and put aside to cool.

Put the oven settings to 350 degrees F.

Cook as you stir onions in hot oil in a skillet over medium fire until tender.

Stir in ham, cooled potatoes, pepper, eggs, and salt for 5 minutes.

Spread cheese on top and bake in the hot oven for 10 minutes.

# 4. Spinach & Potato Frittata

Saturdays are perfect days to enjoy a cool brunch with your family. This potato-spinach loaded frittata will make a perfect meal experience.

**Serving Size:** 6

**Cooking Time:** 20 Minutes

## Ingredients:

- 2 tbsp. olive oil
- 6 sliced red potatoes
- 1 cup torn spinach
- 2 tbsp. sliced green onions
- 1 tsp. crushed garlic
- salt & pepper as desired
- 6 eggs
- ⅓ cup milk
- ½ cup shredded Cheddar cheese

## Instructions:

Heat the oil on medium fire, in a skillet then add the potatoes to cook as you stir for 10 minutes.

Stir in garlic, salt, onions, pepper, and spinach for 2 minutes

In a dish, beat together milk and eggs, then add to the garlic mixture in the skillet.

Spread the cheese on top and cook on low heat while covered for 7 minutes.

# 5. Asparagus and Mushroom Frittata

A hearty frittata filled with nutritious veggies, worth serving the entire family.

**Serving Size:** 6

**Cooking Time:** 50 Minutes

## Ingredients:

- 1 tbsp. butter
- 3 tbsp. olive oil
- ½ lb. chopped asparagus
- ½ lb. sliced mushrooms
- 6 eggs
- 1 tbsp. water
- 1 tsp. chopped thyme
- 3 tbsp. grated Parmesan cheese
- ½ cup shredded mozzarella cheese

## Instructions:

Put the oven settings to 325 degrees F

Using an ovenproof skillet over medium heat, melt the butter, then add olive oil and asparagus to cook as you stir for 10 minutes.

Stir in the mushrooms for 5 minutes.

Mix thyme, water, and eggs in a bowl, then pour into the skillet and cook while covered for 5 minutes on low heat.

Move the skillet to the oven and bake the contents for 15 minutes.

Spread mozzarella cheese and parmesan cheese on top and broil until the cheese melts.

# 6. Cheesy Potato Frittata

Prepare this cheesy frittata filled with shredded potatoes on a Sunday morning and stay energized for hours.

**Serving Size:** 4

**Cooking Time:** 30 Minutes

## Ingredients:

- 2 tbsp. olive oil
- 2 shredded russet potatoes
- 1 diced onion
- salt & pepper as desired
- ½ cup shredded Cheddar cheese
- 4 beaten eggs

## Instructions:

Preheat your oven at 400 degrees F.

Fry the potatoes in a skillet with hot oil over medium heat for 15 minutes.

Add onions, then reduce the heat and cook as you stir until the onions are soft. Add some pepper & salt, then pour the eggs over the onion-potato mixture.

Bring the skillet to the oven and bake for 10 minutes, add cheese on top, then bake for 5 more minutes.

# 7. Sausage Frittata

This is a versatile frittata recipe. You can serve a week-night dinner when you want something quick and delicious at the same time. You can also enjoy it as a satisfying brunch.

**Serving Size:** 8

**Cooking Time:** 30 Minutes

**Ingredients:**

- 9.6 oz. Pork Sausage Crumbles
- 2 cups cooked & cubed red potatoes
- 8 eggs
- ¼ cup grated Parmesan cheese
- ¼ tsp. salt
- ¼ tsp. black pepper
- ½ cup chopped seeded tomato

2 sliced green onions

**Instructions:**

In a cooking casserole, cook the sausages on medium fire for 5 minutes; stir in the potatoes.

In a bowl, whisk cheese, pepper, eggs, and salt, then pour over the potato mixture to cook for 2 minutes.

Put the heat to low, then cook while covered for 15 minutes.

Slice and serve topped with onions and tomato.

# 8. Spinach and Mushroom Frittata

This frittata is all you need to prepare when looking for a perfect recipe loaded with healthy veggies.

**Serving Size:** 6

**Cooking Time:** 30 Minutes

**Ingredients:**

- 10 oz. chopped spinach, thawed and squeezed
- 4 eggs
- 1 cup ricotta cheese
- ¾ cup grated Parmesan cheese
- ¾ cup chopped portobello mushrooms
- ½ cup chopped scallions
- ¼ tsp. dried Italian seasonings
- Salt and pepper as desired
- Cooking spray as needed

**Instructions:**

Put the oven settings to 375 degrees F, then coat a casserole pan with cooking spray

Whisk together all the ingredients, then pour on the ready casserole dish and bake for 30 minutes.

# 9. Banana Frittata

A sweet and nutritious frittata filled with bananas. Perfect for kids and adults too. Apples will also work magic in place of bananas.

**Serving Size:** 3

**Cooking Time:** 15 Minutes

**Ingredients:**

- ½ cup all-purpose flour
- ¼ tsp. salt
- 2 tbsp. white sugar
- ¼ cup milk
- 2 eggs
- 2 sliced ripe bananas
- 2 tbsp. vegetable oil
- ½ tbsp. butter

**Instructions:**

Mix the flour, sugar, & salt in a bowl, then stir in milk gradually until smooth.

Beat in one egg at a time until done, then fold in sliced bananas.

In a nonstick skillet, add oil to heat up, then add the batter to cook on both sides until golden brown

Serve warm sprinkled with sugar.

# 10. Smoked Salmon Frittata

Make sure you serve this recipe while still hot to enjoy every magic in it. You can add some sliced avocado and herbs of your choice for a perfect meal experience.

**Serving Size:** 4

**Cooking Time:** 30 Minutes

**Ingredients:**

- 4 tbsp. olive oil
- ¼ chopped onion
- salt & pepper to taste
- 4 oz. pepper smoked salmon
- 8 chopped black olives
- 6 eggs
- 2 tbsp. milk
- 2 tbsp. heavy cream
- 8 oz. cubed cream cheese

**Instructions:**

Put the oven settings to preheat at 350 degrees F

In an oven-safe dish, heat oil, then add onions, pepper, and salt to cook until soft for 5 minutes.

Stir in olives and salmon for 3 minutes.

Whisk cream, milk, and eggs in a bowl, then pour over the olive mixture, stirring gently.

Add cheese cubes on top and cook over medium heat until firm.

Take the skillet to the oven and bake for 20 minutes.

# 11. Air Fryer Breakfast Frittata

An air fryer will give this frittata a perfect look and texture. Besides, it is quick and easy to prepare for a nutritious breakfast.

**Serving Size:** 2

**Cooking Time:** 20 Minutes

## Ingredients:

- cooking spray as needed
- ¼ lb. cooked and crumbled sausage
- 4 beaten eggs
- ½ cup shredded Cheddar-Monterey Jack cheese blend
- 2 tbsp. diced red bell pepper
- 1 chopped green onion
- ¼ tsp. cayenne pepper

## Instructions:

Put your air fryer to 360 degrees F, then coat a nonstick baking pan with cooking spray.

In a bowl, mic cayenne pepper, green onion, bell pepper, cheese, eggs, and sausage until even, then pour into the baking pan.

Bake in the air fryer for 20 minutes.

# 12. Spinach Loaded Frittata

With ham, spinach, onion, cheese, and bell pepper, you will have this satisfying frittata in a few minutes.

**Serving Size:** 4

**Cooking Time:** 15 Minutes

**Ingredients:**

- 2 tbsp. olive oil
- ½ cup stripped red bell pepper
- ½ cup chopped onion
- 3 eggs
- ½ cup milk
- 10 oz. thawed, squeezed & chopped spinach
- 1 cup cooked & chopped ham
- ½ cup shredded mozzarella cheese
- ½ cup crumbled feta cheese
- ½ tsp. salt
- ¼ tsp. black pepper

**Instructions:**

In a skillet on medium heat, cook as you stir onion and red pepper in hot oil for 5 minutes.

Whisk milk and eggs in a bowl until smooth, then stir in black pepper, feta cheese, salt, mozzarella cheese, ham, and spinach until even, then pour into the skillet.

Cook while covered for 10 minutes.

# 13. Cheesy Chorizo Frittata

You will love this colorful frittata with a perfect tender texture. Easy to make and delicious at the same time

**Serving Size:** 6

**Cooking Time:** 30 Minutes

## Ingredients:

- ¼ lb. crumbled chorizo
- 6 oz. baby spinach leaves
- 2 cups halved cherry tomatoes
- 4 sliced green onions
- 6 eggs
- ½ cup milk
- 1½ cups Shredded Pepper Jack Cheese, divided

## Instructions:

Put the oven settings to preheat at 375 degrees F

In an oven-safe dish, cook as you stir chorizo on medium heat, then remove chorizo, leaving the fats.

Add spinach to the same skillet to cook for 2 minutes, then mic in the onions, cooked chorizo, and tomatoes. Stir gently, then remove from the fire.

In a bowl, whisk milk and eggs, then stir in 1 cup cheese. Stir this mixture into the skillet until even, then top with the remaining cheese.

Bake for 25 minutes.

# 14. Italian Frittata

Salami, artichoke hearts, mushrooms, and cherry tomatoes make up this appetizing frittata! Add some extra spices for that extra aroma!

**Serving Size:** 6

**Cooking Time:** 25 Minutes

**Ingredients:**

- ½ cup diced salami
- ½ cup drained & chopped artichoke hearts
- ½ cup chopped cherry tomatoes
- 4.5 oz. sliced mushrooms, drained
- 6 eggs
- ⅓ cup milk
- 2 chopped green onions
- 1 minced garlic clove
- 1 tsp. dried basil
- 1 tsp. onion powder
- 1 tsp. salt
- Black pepper to taste
- ⅓ cup grated Parmesan cheese
- 1 cup shredded mozzarella cheese

**Instructions:**

Put the oven settings to preheat at 425 degrees F, and butter a baking casserole

In a saucepan over medium heat, cook as you stir salami, mushrooms, tomatoes, and artichokes for 4 minutes. Pour this mixture into the baking casserole.

In a bowl, mix black pepper, onion powder, salt, basil, garlic, green onions, milk, and eggs until even, then pour over the mushroom mixture.

Add parmesan and mozzarella cheese on top and bake for 20 minutes.

# 15. Kale and Fennel Frond Frittata

Transform your kales into an aromatic frittata recipe. All you need to do is add some few more ingredients to make the final frittata colorful and nutritious.

**Serving Size:** 2

**Cooking Time:** 10 Minutes

**Ingredients:**

- 2 tsp. olive oil
- 1 cup chopped kale
- 1/2 cup chopped fennel fronds
- 4 beaten eggs
- salt & black pepper to taste
- 4 oz. crumbled feta cheese

**Instructions:**

Put an oven rack 6 inches from the heat source and preheat the broiler of your oven

Using an oven-proof skillet over medium heat, add oil to heat up, then cook kale for 5 minutes, then stir in fennel fronds for 1 more minute

Add some salt to the beaten eggs, then pour into the skillet, stirring gently.

Add crumbled cheese on top and broil for 10 minutes.

# 16. Artichoke Frittata

Rich in nutrients and delicious, this is an ultimate frittata recipe you need for a cool brunch.

**Serving Size:** 12

**Cooking Time:** 45 Minutes

## Ingredients:

- 12 oz. marinated artichoke hearts
- 1 bunch chopped green onions
- 1 lb. grated Cheddar cheese
- 9 beaten eggs
- 14 crumbled saltine crackers
- ½ cup chopped parsley
- 2 minced garlic cloves
- ¼ tsp. hot pepper sauce
- salt & black pepper as desired

## Instructions:

Put the oven setting to preheat at 325 degrees F. Meanwhile, drain artichokes, putting aside 3 tablespoons of the liquid. Chop the drained artichokes and put aside.

In a large saucepan, heat up the reserved liquid from artichokes, then stir in green onions for 3 minutes.

Pour the green onions into a bowl, then mix in pepper, hot sauce, crackers, salt, garlic, parsley, eggs, cheddar, and artichoke hearts. Pour this mixture into a baking casserole and bake for 40 minutes.

# 17. 3-Cheese Salami Frittata

Unlike many other frittata recipes, you will need to serve this three-cheese salami frittata chilled to enjoy every single bite. It is a perfect snacking or breakfast recipe idea.

**Serving Size:** 8

**Cooking Time:** 30 Minutes

**Ingredients:**

- 16 eggs
- ¼ cup milk
- 1 tbsp. olive oil
- 6 1/4-inch thick slices Genoa salami
- 1 cup chopped parsley
- ½ cup grated Parmesan cheese, divided
- ½ cup grated Romano cheese, divided
- ½ cup shredded mozzarella cheese, divided
- salt & black pepper to taste
- ¼ tsp. red pepper flakes

**Instructions:**

Put the oven settings to preheat at 425 degrees F, then whisk together milk and eggs in a bowl.

In an ovenproof casserole, heat oil, then add ½ of the egg mixture, then salami, parsley, 2/3 of the parmesan cheese, 2/3 of the Romano cheese, 2/3 of the mozzarella cheese, red pepper flakes, pepper, and salt.

Cook for about 15 minutes, then add the remaining egg mixture, then the remaining parmesan, Romano, mozzarella cheese, some more pepper, salt, and red pepper flakes.

Bake in the oven for 25 minutes

Slice, then chill the slices for 1 hour before serving.

# 18. Halloumi and Zucchini Frittata

Filled with fresh herbs, you will enjoy every single bite of this halloumi frittata.

**Serving Size:** 2

**Cooking Time:** 15 Minutes

## Ingredients:

- 1 tbsp. olive oil
- 1 grated and squeezed zucchini
- salt & black pepper to taste
- 1 tbsp. chopped mint
- 1 tbsp. chopped dill
- 4 eggs
- 4 oz. sliced halloumi cheese

## Instructions:

In an ovenproof skillet, heat oil, then add zucchini and salt to cook as you stir for 5 minutes. Mix in dill and mint for 1 minute.

Whisk some pepper, eggs, and some salt in a bowl, then add to the skillet with zucchini mixture, stirring gently for 2 minutes, until set.

Put an oven rack about 6 inches from direct heat and heat the broiler.

Add halloumi slices over the frittata, then broil for 5 minutes.

# 19. Frittata with Leftover Greens

Are you wondering what to do with your leftover greens? Worry not. Here is a perfect frittata, tasty and nutritious at the same time.

**Serving Size:** 6

**Cooking Time:** 20 Minutes

## Ingredients:

- 5 eggs
- 2 egg whites
- 2 tbsp. chopped parsley
- ¼ tsp. salt
- ¼ tsp. black pepper
- 1 tbsp. olive oil
- 1 cup chopped red onion
- ¼ tsp. salt
- ¼ tsp. black pepper
- ¼ cup halved grape tomatoes
- 1 cup cooked Swiss chard
- ¼ cup grated Parmesan cheese

## Instructions:

Put the oven's rack 6 inches from direct heat and preheat the broiler.

In a bowl, beat together egg whites and eggs, then blend in ¼ tsp pepper, ¼ tsp salt, and ¼ tsp parsley.

Using a cast-iron skillet set over medium heat, add oil to heat up, then add onion, ¼ tsp pepper, and ¼ tsp salt to cook as you stir for 5 minutes.

Stir in tomatoes for 1 minute, then cook Swiss chard until hot. Pour the egg mixture to the skillet to cook while covered until set for 5 minutes.

Add parmesan cheese on top, then broil for 2 minutes.

# 20. Microwave Frittata

Did you know that, with a microwave, you can have an amazing breakfast idea in minutes? Well, try this special frittata recipe in your microwave before stepping out!

**Serving Size:** 1

**Cooking Time:** 5 Minutes

**Ingredients:**

- cooking spray as desired
- 2 eggs
- 1 tbsp. pesto
- 2 tbsp. ricotta cheese
- 2 tbsp. grated Parmesan cheese
- black pepper to taste
- 1 tbsp. chopped green onion

**Instructions:**

In a large coffee mug, coat some cooking spray in it

In a bowl, whisk together pepper, parmesan cheese, ricotta cheese, pesto, and eggs, the pour into the mug.

Cook in the microwave for 90 seconds, stirring after every 30 seconds.

Serve the frittata garnished with green onions.

# 21. Asparagus Frittata

If you have eggs in your kitchen, then you can cook a frittata at any given moment with a wide range of ingredients. Here is an asparagus-loaded frittata you can try out!

**Serving Size:** 4

**Cooking Time:** 20 Minutes

## Ingredients:

- 1 tbsp. olive oil
- 2 tsp. butter
- ½ lb. trimmed asparagus
- 8 eggs
- ½ cup grated Parmesan cheese
- 7 tbsp. milk
- salt & black pepper to taste
- 1 tbsp. chopped parsley

## Instructions:

In a nonstick pan set on medium heat, heat up the oil, then cook as you stir asparagus for 15 minutes.

Whisk the eggs until foamy, then mix in milk, pepper, parmesan cheese, and salt. Pour this mixture over the asparagus and cook for 15 more minutes.

Serve garnished with parsley.

# 22. Rosemary, Bacon, and Tomato Frittata

Rosemary flavor gives this incredible frittata the best taste and aroma, perfect for serving during special occasions.

**Serving Size:** 6

**Cooking Time:** 50 Minutes

**Ingredients:**

- 1 lb. diced red potatoes
- 12 eggs
- 1 cup grated Parmesan cheese
- ¾ cup milk
- 1 tbsp. minced rosemary, divided
- salt & black pepper to taste
- 6 oz. chopped bacon
- 1 diced tomato

**Instructions:**

Put the oven settings to preheat at 375 degrees F

Microwave the potatoes as you stir for 3 minutes

In a bowl, mix ½ of the rosemary, milk, parmesan cheese, pepper, eggs, and salt

In an oven-safe casserole, cook the bacon until crisp for 5 minutes, then set aside ¼ cup of the bacon and drain excess fats from the casserole.

Add potatoes in the casserole with bacon drippings along with the bacon drippings for 2 minutes, then remove from the fire.

Mix in the tomato and egg mixture then sprinkle reserved bacon, and the remaining rosemary on top.

Bake for 40 minutes.

# 23. Ham and Cheese Frittata

You don't want to miss a satisfying, yet nutritious meal experience on your next picnic. Make this soft and aromatic frittata and enjoy every single bite.

**Serving Size:** 4

**Cooking Time:** 25 Minutes

## Ingredients:

- 3 eggs
- 3 tbsp. milk
- 2 tbsp. butter
- 2 cubed potatoes
- ½ cup cooked & cubed ham
- ¼ cup chopped onion
- 1½ tsp. minced garlic
- ¼ cup water
- salt & black pepper to taste
- ¼ cup shredded Cheddar cheese

## Instructions:

Put the oven rack 6 inches away from direct heat and start preheating the broiler.

Whisk milk and eggs in a bowl, leave aside.

In an oven-safe casserole set over medium heat, heat up the butter, then add garlic, salt, onion, ham, pepper, and potatoes to cook as you stir for 15 minutes, adding water as needed

Add the egg-milk mixture, then cook until set.

Broil in the hot oven for 5 minutes, add cheddar cheese and broil for 5 more minutes.

# 24. Air-Fried Greek Yogurt Frittata

Fresh spinach, eggs, and Greek yogurt gives this frittatas a health branch for anyone. When prepared in the air-frier, the texture is just perfect and the color eye-catching.

**Serving Size:** 2

**Cooking Time:** 25 Minutes

## Ingredients:

- ½ tsp. olive oil
- 2 tbsp. minced onion
- 2 tbsp. minced carrot
- 2 tbsp. minced celery
- 2 tbsp. minced Italian parsley
- 8 oz. baby spinach leaves
- 4 eggs
- ⅓ cup nonfat plain Greek yogurt
- 1 tsp. black pepper
- ½ tsp. red pepper flakes

## Instructions:

Set a nonstick baking pan in the air-fryer and set it to preheat at 350 degrees F.

Once the baking pan is hot, remove it carefully, then add oil, parsley, celery, carrot, and onion.

Add the pan back to the ai fryer and cook for 5 minutes.

Chop ½ of the spinach and mix it in a bowl along with black pepper, Greek yogurt, and eggs. Add this mixture into the baking pan and mix gently.

Cook in the air fryer for 18 minutes.

Once cooled, serve sprinkled with the remaining spinach leaves and pepper flakes.

# 25. Cheesy Rice and Zucchini Frittata

This is a perfect frittata to make, especially if you are having some leftover rice and don't know what to do with it. You can even serve it for a satisfying lunch and enjoy it with your family.

**Serving Size:** 6

**Cooking Time:** 35 Minutes

**Ingredients:**

- Cooking spray as needed
- 5 sliced zucchinis
- 2 cups cooked basmati rice
- ¼ cup shredded Havarti cheese
- ¼ cup shredded Parmesan cheese
- 1 cup milk
- 4 eggs, separated, divided
- 2 tsp. Sriracha sauce
- 1 tsp. salt
- ½ tsp. black pepper
- ¼ cup panko bread crumbs

**Instructions:**

Put the oven settings to preheat at 350 degrees F and coat a baking casserole with cooking spray.

In a bowl, mix parmesan, Havarti, cooked rice, and zucchini. Whisk together sriracha, pepper, egg yolks, salt, and milk in a small bowl, then mix into the rice mixture until even.

Beat the whites until stiff, then blend into the rice mixture and pour the whole mixture into the ready baking casserole.

Bake for 25 minutes, add panko and bake for 10 more minutes.

# 26. Roast Beef and Cheddar Frittata

When you want something unique, tasty, and nutritious, then go for this frittata loaded with roast beef and some cheese.

**Serving Size:** 4

**Cooking Time:** 45 Minutes

**Ingredients:**

- Cooking spray as needed
- 10 beaten eggs
- 10.5 oz. condensed cream of mushroom soup
- 2 cups shredded Cheddar cheese
- 8 oz. deli-style chopped roast beef
- ½ tsp. black pepper

**Instructions:**

Put the oven settings to preheat at 350 degrees F, then coat a baking casserole with cooking spray.

Mix cream of mushroom soup and eggs, then stir in black pepper, roast beef, and cheddar cheese.

Bake for 50 minutes.

# 27. Broccoli-Cheddar Frittata

A frittata will give you a perfect way to blend your veggies into a tasty meal. Do you enjoy broccoli? Here is your ultimate frittata!

**Serving Size:** 8

**Cooking Time:** 15 Minutes

**Ingredients:**

- 7 eggs
- ¼ cup heavy cream
- 1 tsp. smoked paprika
- salt & black pepper to taste
- 2 tbsp. unsalted butter
- ½ cup chopped onion
- 1½ cups chopped broccoli
- 1 cup thawed diced hash brown potatoes
- 1 cup shredded Cheddar cheese
- 4 slices cooked & crumbled bacon

**Instructions:**

Put the oven rack in the center and put the oven settings to preheat at 400 degrees F.

Whisk together pepper, smoked paprika, cream, salt, and eggs, then put aside.

In an oven-safe casserole, heat up the butter on medium heat, then add onions to cook for 2 minutes. Stir in the broccoli for 2 minutes, then potatoes along with some pepper and salt for 2 minutes

Put off the heat, sprinkle cheese and bacon on top, then pour the egg mixture over the veggies, shaking gently.

Bake in the ready oven for 10 minutes.

# 28. Slow Cooker Frittata

If you are a vegetarian, then this frittata favors you for that perfect breakfast meal idea. You can as well include some sausages if you aren't a vegetarian and want something super tasty.

**Serving Size:** 6

**Cooking Time:** 65 Minutes

**Ingredients:**

- cooking spray as needed
- 1 tsp. ghee
- 8 oz. sliced mushrooms
- ¼ cup chopped spinach
- ¼ cup sliced cherry tomatoes
- 2 sliced green onions
- salt & black pepper as desired
- 6 eggs
- ½ cup shredded Cheddar cheese
- 2 tbsp. chopped parsley
- 1 tbsp. grated Parmesan cheese
- 2 tsp. Italian seasoning

**Instructions:**

Coat the slow cooker with enough cooking spray

In a cooking casserole over medium heat, heat up the ghee, then add green onion, tomatoes, spinach, and mushroom to cook for 5 minutes. Add some pepper and salt, then pour into the slow cooker.

In a bowl, combine Italian seasoning, parmesan cheese, parsley, cheddar cheese, and eggs, then add into the slow cooker, then cook for 4 hours on low or 2 hours on high.

# 29. Zucchini Scallion Frittata Cups

These protein-packed frittata cups are a perfect option for anyone leaving a busy lifestyle. They are perfect for freezing too, making it easy to meal-plan ahead.

**Serving Size:** 12

**Cooking Time:** 30 Minutes

## Ingredients:

- Cooking spray as needed
- 7 egg whites
- 3 eggs
- 2 tbsp. half and-half
- 2 cups shredded zucchini
- 1 cup chopped green onion
- 3 tbsp. grated Parmigiano-Reggiano cheese

## Instructions:

Put the oven settings to preheat at 350 degrees F, then coat 12 muffin tins with cooking spray.

In a bowl, whisk together half-and-half, eggs, and egg whites until even, then stir in cheese, green onion, and zucchini.

Add this mixture into the muffin tins and bake for 35 minutes.

# 30. Radish Green Frittata

Serve this aromatic frittata when still hot with a splash of your best hot sauce. It also makes perfect sandwich ideas.

**Serving Size:** 4

**Cooking Time:** 20 Minutes

## Ingredients:

- 1 tbsp. olive oil
- 2 oz. chopped leeks
- 1 bunch raw radish greens
- 8 eggs
- 4 tbsp. grated Parmesan cheese
- 2 tbsp. heavy whipping cream
- 4 shredded radishes

## Instructions:

In an oven-proof casserole, heat up the oil, then cook as you stir leeks for 5 minutes. Stir in radish tops for 5 more minutes.

Put the oven rack 6 inches away from direct heat and preheat the broiler.

In a bowl, whisk together heavy cream, parmesan cheese, and eggs, then add into the leek mixture to cook on low heat while covered for 10 minutes.

Broil in the ready oven for 5 minutes, then serve topped with shredded radishes.

# 31. Potato and Zucchini Frittata

You can enjoy this frittata for a quick dinner, a perfect lunch, a healthy brunch, or a satisfying breakfast. Feel free to include varied veggies and bacon as preferred.

**Serving Size:** 4

**Cooking Time:** 20 Minutes

## Ingredients:

- 2 cooked and cubed potatoes
- 1 tbsp. olive oil
- 2 sliced zucchinis
- 1 chopped onion
- 8 eggs
- 1 tsp. dried oregano
- 1 tsp. cayenne pepper
- salt & black pepper to taste

## Instructions:

In a cast-iron skillet set on medium fire, heat up the oil, then fry the onion and zucchini for 7 minutes, then stir in the cooked potatoes.

In a bowl, whisk together pepper, eggs, salt, cayenne pepper, and oregano until even, then add to the skillet to cook for 10 minutes.

Put the oven rack in the center and broil the frittata for 5 minutes.

# 32. Mini Frittata Muffins

When you get unexpected guests, prepare these tasty and flavorful mini frittatas in muffin cups and enjoy the moment. You will only need bell peppers, tomatoes, cheese, and eggs for that extra flavor. They also make a perfect lunch, besides being the best breakfast recipe.

**Serving Size:** 6

**Cooking Time:** 20 Minutes

**Ingredients:**

- Cooking spray as desired
- 12 eggs
- 2 tbsp. milk
- 2 tsp. salt
- 2 tsp. black pepper
- 1 chopped tomato
- 1 chopped green bell pepper
- 2 cups shredded Colby-Jack cheese

**Instructions:**

Put the oven settings to preheat at 395 degrees F, then coat a muffin pan with cooking spray.

Mix pepper, eggs, salt, and milk

Add tomatoes and green peppers evenly among the muffin tins, then top equal amounts of Colby-jack cheese.

Stir egg mixture gently into each muffin tin, then bake for 20 minutes.

# 33. Quinoa Mini Frittatas

Another recipe loaded with healthy ingredients for a frittata you can serve for dinner, lunch, brunch, or breakfast.

**Serving Size:** 6

**Cooking Time:** 45 Minutes

**Ingredients:**

- 1½ cups water
- 1 cup shredded Swiss cheese
- 2 cups cooked quinoa
- 2 eggs
- 2 egg whites
- 1 cup shredded zucchini
- ¼ cup chopped parsley
- 2 tbsp. grated Parmesan cheese
- ½ cup diced ham
- ¼ tsp. white pepper

**Instructions:**

Put the oven settings to preheat at 400 degrees F, then butter 6 muffin tins.

Mix all the ingredients until even, then fill into the muffin tins and bake for 30 minutes.

# 34. Swiss & Ham Mini Frittatas

Easy to make, yet delicious and nutritious frittatas perfect for snacking You can't afford to miss this recipe!

**Serving Size:** 8

**Cooking Time:** 15 Minutes

**Ingredients:**

- Cooking spray as needed
- 6 slices chopped Swiss cheese
- 6 slices chopped deli ham
- 8 eggs
- ½ tsp. onion powder
- ½ tsp. garlic powder
- ¼ tsp. black pepper

**Instructions:**

Put the oven settings to preheat at 375 degrees F and coat a 24-mini muffin pan with cooking spray.

Mix ham and cheese, then add equal portions in the muffin tins.

In a bowl, whisk together pepper, onion powder, eggs, and garlic powder, then add equal portions in the muffin tins.

Bake in the ready oven for 12 minutes.

# 35. Shrimp Frittata

Everyone deserves a protein-loaded snack or brunch at any given time. If you enjoy shrimps, here is a quick recipe for you.

**Serving Size:** 4

**Cooking Time:** 12 Minutes

## Ingredients:

- ½ lb. chopped shrimp
- 6 eggs
- 2 tbsp. torn basil leaves
- 1/4 cup chopped sun-dried tomatoes
- Salt & black pepper as desired
- 2 tbsp. butter
- 4 chopped scallions

## Instructions:

Beat the eggs, then mix in tomatoes, salt, basil, black pepper, and shrimp in a large bowl.

Preheat the broiler, then melt 2 tablespoons of butter in an oven-safe casserole.

Cook the scallions for 2 minutes, then add the egg mixture to cook on low heat for 10 minutes while covered.

Broil for 2 minutes, then serve hot.

# 36. Squash, pea & feta mini frittatas

Are you looking for a perfect picnic meal idea? Well, you will never go wrong with these mini frittatas packed with varied veggies for that perfect taste and color.

**Serving Size:** 8

**Cooking Time:** 25 Minutes

**Ingredients:**

- 1 oz. peeled and cubed butternut squash
- 1 oz. frozen peas
- 3½ crumbled feta
- 4 eggs
- Salt & pepper as desired

**Instructions:**

Put the oven settings to preheat at 200 degrees F, then microwave butternut cubes on high for 7 minutes, until soft.

Fill the parchment paper into 8 muffin tins; allow to overhang

Add equal portions of peas, squash, and feta among the muffin tins

Whisk the eggs, pepper, & salt, then add into the muffin tins and bake them for 20 minutes in the ready oven.

# 37. Prawn & leek frittata

Prawns too, will give you irresistible frittatas. The taste, the color, and the nutritional value are all just perfect for someone looking for that unique recipe to serve with a salad or bread.

**Serving Size:** 2

**Cooking Time:** 16 Minutes

**Ingredients:**

- 3 sliced leeks
- 5 oz. raw peeled king prawns
- 5 eggs
- Salt & pepper as desired
- 4oz. garlic & herb cream cheese

**Instructions:**

In a casserole dish, heat 2 tbsp. oil, then add the leeks to cook for 5 minutes.

Stir in the prawns for 1 minute.

Whisk together ½ of the cream cheese and eggs, pepper, & salt, then add to the leek mixture

Dot the remaining cheese on top, then cook for 8 minutes on medium heat.

Grill for 2 minutes on a heated grill for a perfect finishing.

# 38. Pea & pasta frittata

If you have any leftover pasta dish, try making this frittata recipe and blend in some mint for that extra flavor. You will love everything about this recipe!

**Serving Size:** 4

**Cooking Time:** 15 Minutes

## Ingredients:

- 5 eggs
- ¾ cup milk
- 80g grated parmesan
- 7 oz. cooked pasta shells
- ½ pack chopped mint
- 200g frozen peas
- Black pepper and salt as desired
- 1 tbsp butter
- Green salad as needed, to serve

## Instructions:

Preheat your grill on high, then whisk together eggs, black pepper, peas, cooked pasta, salt, mint, and ½ of the cheese.

In an oven-safe casserole, heat the butter over medium heat, then add the pasta mixture to cook for 5 minutes until set.

Add the remaining cheese on top and grill for 10 minutes.

Slice and serve with your preferred green salad.

# 39. Apple and Leek Frittata

You will enjoy every single bite of this perfect frittata. Make sure you slice the apples thinly for amazing results.

**Serving Size:** 4

**Cooking Time:** 30 Minutes

**Ingredients:**

- 4 eggs
- 4 egg whites
- 1 sliced apple
- 1 sliced leek
- 1 tbsp. chopped sage
- sage leaf as desired for garnishing
- cooking spray as needed
- salt & pepper as desired

**Instructions:**

Whisk egg whites and eggs in a bowl, then put aside.

In a skillet placed on medium heat, add some cooking spray, then cook the leeks for 2 minutes.

Stir in the apples for 3 minutes, then add some salt, sage, and black pepper.

Add the egg mixture into the skillet, then cook for 6 minutes while covered on low heat.

Serve garnished with sage leaves as desired.

# 40. Crab Frittata

Until you have a bite of this healthy frittata, you will never think of any other brunch recipe, especially on special occasions.

**Serving Size:** 2

**Cooking Time:** 25 Minutes

**Ingredients:**

- 5 eggs
- 1/3 cup cream
- ½ tsp. grated lemon rind
- Tabasco sauce to taste
- salt & black pepper as desired
- 3 tbsp. grated sharp cheddar cheese
- 1 diced potato
- 1 diced onion
- 1 tbsp. oil
- ¼ cup diced red bell pepper
- 1 cup crab meat

**Instructions:**

In a bowl, combine black pepper, tabasco sauce, salt, lemon rind, cream, and eggs, then put aside.

Cook the potato and onion in a microwave for 3 minutes

In a skillet placed on medium heat, add oil, then cook the onion and potatoes until brown, then stir in the bell pepper.

Add this mixture over the egg mixture, then sprinkle crab meat on top.

Cook for 5 minutes, then broil for a few minutes until browned on top.

# Conclusion

Thank you for reading up to this end. If you've always wondered what frittatas are and why they make great meals, then this cookbook has answered all your concerns as far as frittatas are concerned.

What's more, I hope you've learned and discovered that making frittatas isn't a hassle. Most of the ingredients are readily available, and what is even more fascinating is that you can transform a wide range of ingredients into a sumptuous frittata. Be it leftover pasta, you can always have a plan. Whether you are having any leftover veggies and don't know what to do with them, making a frittata is the perfect solution!

Having included the forty best frittata recipe ideas, you can set a cooking pace and start making different frittatas on different days for different occasions. All you need is to follow the simplified steps, master the processes, and become a pro in making tasty and flavorful frittatas.

With this said, why wait? Use this cookbook and become an expert in your own kitchen. Turn those ingredients into delightful frittata by making this cookbook your kitchen companion.

# Appendices

## Thank you ♥

Hey, guys! I just wanted to say thanks for supporting me by purchasing one of my e-books. I have to say—when I first started writing cookbooks, I didn't have many expectations for myself because it was never a part of "the plan." It was more of a hobby, something I did for me and decided to put out there if someone might click on my book and buy it because they liked my food. Well, let me just say it's been a while since those days, and it's been a wild journey!

Now, cookbook writing is a huge part of my life, and I'm doing things I love! So, THANK YOU for trusting me with your weekly meal preps, weekend BBQs, 10-minute dinners, and all of your special occasions. If it weren't for you, I wouldn't be able to concentrate on producing all sorts of delicious recipes, which is why I've decided to reach out and ask for your help. What kind of recipes would you like to see more of? Are you interested in special diets, foods made with kitchen appliances, or just easy recipes on a time-crunch? Your input will help me create books you want to read with recipes you'll actually make! Make sure to let me know, and your suggestions could trigger an idea for my next book…

Take care!

Owen

Made in United States
North Haven, CT
11 January 2025